The Countries

Germany

Bob Italia

ABDO Publishing Company

visit us at
www.abdopub.com

Published by ABDO Publishing Company, 4940 Viking Drive, Edina, Minnesota 55435.
Copyright © 2002 by Abdo Consulting Group, Inc. International copyrights reserved in
all countries. No part of this book may be reproduced in any form without written
permission from the publisher.

Printed in the United States.

Photo Credits: Corbis
Art Direction & Maps: Neil Klinepier

Library of Congress Cataloging-in-Publication Data

Italia, Bob, 1955-
   Germany / Bob Italia.
      p. cm. -- (The countries)
Includes index.
Summary: Provides an overview of the history, geography, people, economy,
government, and other aspects of life in Germany.
ISBN 1-57765-753-5
1. Germany--Juvenile literature. [1. Germany.] I. Title. II. Series.

  DD17 .I85 2002
  943--dc21

2001040912

Contents

Hallo!

Hello from Germany, a country with more people than any other European country except Russia.

Long ago, tribal peoples traveled from northern Europe into what is now Germany. Tribes became kingdoms, and kingdoms became empires. In recent times, Germany was a divided nation. It now has become an **economic** power.

Germany has low, flat plains and mountainous regions. Because it is near the sea, it has a mild climate.

Since it is a highly industrialized nation, Germany does not have much natural vegetation. But Germany has a variety of wildlife, including game animals.

Most of the people living in Germany were born there. Most non-Germans are from Turkey, Yugoslavia, and Italy. Most Germans live in cities. Lutherans make up the largest religious **denomination**.

Germany, a federal **republic**, has many important industrial cities. Berlin, Germany's capital and largest city, is a **cultural**, economic, and political center of

Europe. Manufacturing is the most important part of Germany's **economy**. Trains and automobiles are the most important means of transportation in the country.

Most of Germany's cities and towns have festivals that celebrate music, film, and arts. Many religious festivals are also national holidays.

Germany's varied landscape is ideal for outdoor activities. Soccer is the most popular organized sport.

Germany has many important museums. And Germans have made important contributions to world **culture** and science.

German children in traditional Bavarian costume

Fast Facts

BERLIN

OFFICIAL NAME: Bundesrepublik Deutschland (Federal Republic of Germany)
CAPITAL: Berlin

LAND
- Mountain Range: The Alps
- Highest Peak: Zugspitze 9,721 feet (2,963 m)
- Major Rivers: Rhine, Danube, Elbe, Weser, Oder

PEOPLE
- Population: 82,286,000 (2002 est.)
- Major Cities: Berlin, Hamburg, Munich
- Language: German
- Religions: Lutheranism, Roman Catholicism, Judaism

GOVERNMENT
- Form: Federal republic
- Head of State: Federal president
- Head of Government: Federal chancellor
- Legislature: Parliament
- National Anthem: Third stanza of "Deutschland-Lied" ("Song of Germany")

ECONOMY
- Agricultural Products: Barley, potatoes, sugar beets, wheat; beef cattle, hogs, milk
- Manufactured Products: Chemicals and medicines, electrical equipment, machinery, motor vehicles, processed foods and beverages, steel
- Mining Products: Coal
- Money: Deutsche mark and euro (100 pfennige = 1 Deutsche mark, 100 cents = 1 euro)

The German flag

The German Deutsche mark

Timeline

1000 B.C.	Tribal peoples travel to Germany
100s	Tribes reach the northern edge of the Roman Empire
A.D. 9	Tribes defeat the Romans
400s	Tribes break up the Western Roman Empire
768	Charlemagne establishes the Frankish capital in Aachen
843	Charlemagne's empire is divided into three kingdoms, one for each of his grandsons
1138	Hohenstaufen dynasty comes to power
1273	Rudolf I of Habsburg comes to power
1438	The Habsburgs come to power
1871	Otto von Bismarck unites Germany
1914 to 1918	World War I; Germany is defeated
1933	Adolf Hitler and his Nazi Party establish a dictatorship
1939 to 1945	World War II; Germany is defeated
1961	East Germany builds the Berlin Wall
1989	Germans call for reunification of Germany; the Berlin Wall is opened
1990	East Germany holds elections; the non-Communists gain control of the government; East and West Germany combine their economies; reunification becomes official; the first national elections are held

History

About 1000 B.C., tribal peoples traveled from northern Europe into what is now Germany. They included the Germani, Cimbri, Franks, Goths, and Vandals.

By the 100s B.C., the tribes had reached the northern edge of the **Roman Empire**. The Romans called all the tribes Germani and their land Germania.

In A.D. 9, the Romans tried to conquer these tribes. But the tribes defeated the Romans. In the 400s, the Germanic tribes attacked Rome and broke up the Romans' western empire into smaller kingdoms. The Franks established the largest and most important kingdom.

King Charlemagne

In 768, King Charlemagne established the Frankish capital in Aachen and expanded the kingdom. In 800, Pope Leo III made him Roman emperor.

In 843, Charlemagne's empire was divided into three kingdoms, one for each of his grandsons. By 911, the German kingdom had been divided into five territories: Bavaria, Lorraine, Franconia, Saxony, and Swabia.

The Hohenstaufen **dynasty** came to power in 1138. But by the mid-1200s, the emperors were almost powerless. In 1273, Rudolf I of Habsburg came to power. He seized Austria and made it his main territory.

After Rudolf, other family dynasties ruled Germany. In 1438, the Habsburg family came to power. They ruled until 1806.

For the next two hundred years, Germany was split into many different states, including the kingdom of Prussia. During the late 1800s, Prussia's **prime minister**,

Otto von Bismarck

Adolf Hitler

Otto von Bismarck, united most of these states under his leadership. In 1871, he combined the states into one German empire.

German attempts to expand their territory led to World War I in 1914. Germany was defeated in 1918. Germany then fell into a time of political and **economic** trouble.

In 1933, Adolf Hitler and his Nazi Party established a **dictatorship** and built Germany into a military power. In 1939, Hitler started World War II when Germany attacked Poland. The **Allies** finally defeated Germany in 1945.

Germany was divided into West Germany and East Germany. West Germany became a **democracy** with ties to Western Europe and the

United States. East Germany became a **Communist dictatorship** with ties to the Soviet Union. West Germany became a leading industrial power. East Germany's **economy** eventually grew strong, too.

In 1961, the East German government built a wall through Berlin. The government wanted to stop East Germans from moving to West Germany.

A guard patrols the Berlin Wall.

Helmut Kohl

In 1989, East Germans called for the reunification of East and West Germany. In November, the government opened the Berlin Wall. Non-**Communist** political parties were permitted to form. In March 1990, East Germany held elections. The non-Communists gained control of the government.

In July 1990, East and West Germany combined their **economies**. On October 3, reunification became official. In December, the first national elections were held. West German **chancellor**, Helmut Kohl, became chancellor of a unified Germany. Kohl won again in 1994.

In the election of 1998, Kohl was defeated after 16 years in power. Gerhard Schröder became Germany's

chancellor. Under his leadership, Germany maintained its position as one of Western Europe's most powerful countries.

Gerhard Schröder

The Land

Germany has five main land regions. These regions are the North German Plain, the Central Highlands, the South German Hills, the Black Forest, and the Bavarian Alps.

The low and flat North German Plain is the largest land region in Germany. The region has many rivers that flow into the North or Baltic Seas. These rivers include the Elbe, Ems, Oder, Rhine, and Weser. The southern edge of the Plain has fertile soil called loess.

The Central Highlands have **plateaus** and mountains. The Harz Mountains and the Thuringian Forest have peaks that rise more than 3,000 feet (910 m). The rivers in the Central Highlands, including the Rhine, have steep, narrow valleys.

The South German Hills have fertile lowlands lined by **escarpments**. Much of the region is drained by the Rhine, the Main, and the Neckar Rivers. The Danube River flows through the southern part.

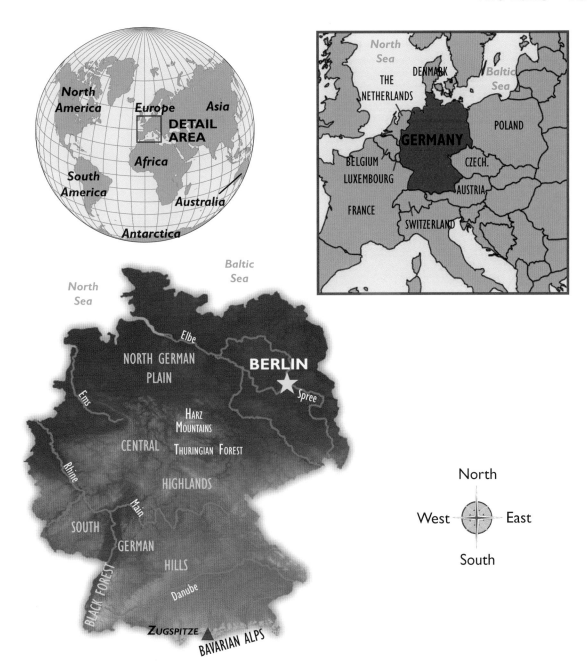

The Black Forest is a mountainous region. It is named after the thick forests of fir and spruce trees that blanket the mountainsides. The region also has deep, narrow valleys.

In the snow-capped Bavarian Alps is the highest point in Germany. Its a 9,721-foot (2,963-m) peak named *Zugspitze*. The Alps also have many lakes and mountain streams that flow into the Danube River.

Because it is near the sea, Germany has a mild climate. West winds from the sea help keep Germany warm in winter and cool in summer. Winters are colder and summers are warmer in the south.

A small lake in the Bavarian Alps

Rainfall

AVERAGE YEARLY RAINFALL

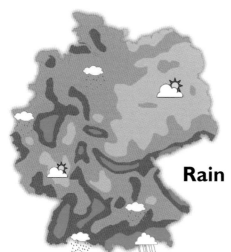

Inches		Centimeters
Under 24		Under 60
24 - 32		60 - 80
32 - 40		80 - 100
Over 40		Over 100

Rain

Temperature

AVERAGE TEMPERATURE

Fahrenheit		Celsius
Over 68°		Over 20°
64° - 68°		18° - 20°
60° - 64°		16° - 18°
46° - 60°		8° - 16°
32° - 46°		0° - 8°
28° - 32°		-2° - 0°
24° - 28°		-4° - -2°
Below 24°		Below -4°

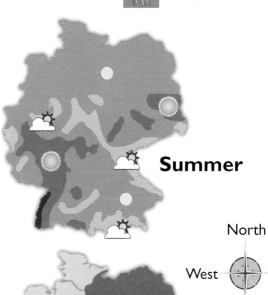

Summer

North
West — East
South

Winter

Plants & Animals

Before people settled Germany, its land was almost totally forested, except for its marshland. But heavy industry has taken its toll on Germany's land. The country has little naturally growing vegetation. Even its forests were planted by people.

The beech tree is common in the Central Highlands. Pine is found in the lowlands and spruce in the uplands. Other **conifers**, such as the Douglas and Sitka spruce, Weymouth pine, and Japanese larch, have been introduced in recent years. Mixed forests are in the highest elevations of the Alps.

Germany has a variety of wildlife, including game animals such as deer, quail, pheasant, chamois, ibex, and wild boar. The polecat, marten, weasel, beaver, and badger are found in the central and southern highlands.

The lynx has reappeared near the Czech Republic border. The elk and wolf are found in the east. Common reptiles include salamanders, slowworms, and various lizards and snakes.

The white-tailed eagle can be found in the North German Plain. The golden eagle can be seen in the Alps. And the white stork is found in and near marshlands.

A beech tree

Germans

Germany has the second-largest population in Europe. Only Russia has more people. Most of the people living in Germany were born there. Most non-Germans are from Turkey, Yugoslavia, and Italy.

The German language has two main forms. High German is spoken in the south and center. Low German is spoken in the north. There are also many dialects in different regions and cities. Government institutions, businesses, newspapers, and radio and television stations use High German.

Most Germans live in cities. Pollution and housing shortages are major problems. Most people live in crowded apartment buildings. Housing in some areas consists of single-family homes and modern condominiums. Other areas have large housing projects. In rural areas, farms are small and are family-owned.

Germans often eat their main meal at noon. Veal, pork, beef, and chicken are popular. Common vegetables include beets, carrots, onions, potatoes, and turnips. A light supper often consists of bread, cheese, and sausage. Beer and wine are popular beverages.

Germany has many world-famous dishes. Sauerkraut was developed to preserve cabbage. Meat

Sausages, soup, and beer

is soaked in vinegar and spices to make a dish called sauerbraten. The Germans are also famous for bratwurst and frankfurters. Well-known cheeses include Limburger, Muenster, and Tilsiter, which are named after the regions from which they come.

Lutherans make up the largest religious **denomination** in Germany. One out of three Germans is Roman Catholic. There are also some Muslims.

Before World War II, about 560,000 Jews lived in Germany. By the end of the war, most Jews had been killed by the Nazis in **concentration camps**. Others fled the country. Today, about 70,000 Jews live in Germany.

Auschwitz-Birkenau, Poland, was the largest Nazi concentration camp in operation during World War II.

Marzipan
German Candies

1 pound almonds, shelled, blanched
1 pound confectioners' sugar
1 egg white, unbeaten

Rose water or orange water
food colors

Carefully dry the shelled almonds, then grind to a powder in an electric blender. Blend almonds, sugar, egg white, and just enough rose water or orange water to make a stiff dough.

Knead with fingers, then place on board dusted with confectioners' sugar and form into desired shapes. Tint with food coloring. Balls of marzipan may be rubbed in chocolate dots or colored sugar. If dough becomes too stiff, work in a little lemon juice, rose water or orange water, adding drop by drop.

When candies are shaped, dry thoroughly in a cool, airy place for 24 hours, then wrap separately or place in a container (such as a little straw basket for fruit) and cover completely with plastic wrap. Makes 2 pounds of candy.

AN IMPORTANT NOTE TO THE CHEF: Always have an adult help with the preparation and cooking of food. Never use kitchen utensils or appliances without adult permission and supervision.

English	German
Yes	Ja (YAH)
No	Nein (NINE)
Please	Bitte (BIH-teh)
Thank You	Danke (DAHN-keh)
Hello	Hallo (hah-LOH)
Goodbye	Auf Wiedersehen (awf VEE-der-zay-ehn)

LANGUAGE

An elementary school student

Starting at age 6, all German children must go to school full-time for at least 9 or 10 years. First they attend *Grundschule* or elementary school for four years. Then some go to *Gymnasium*, which is similar to a junior and senior high school that prepares them for college.

Other students go to *Realschule*, which provides students with **academics** and job training. Still other children attend *Hauptschulen,* or **vocational** schools. These have even fewer academics, but offer much job training.

Germany has about 60 universities. The University of Heidelberg is Germany's oldest university.

One of the buildings of the University of Heidelberg

The Economy

Manufacturing is the most important part of Germany's **economy**. Germany has several major manufacturing regions. The Ruhr region is the country's most important. It includes the manufacturing centers of Dortmund, Duisburg, and Düsseldorf.

The Ruhr produces most of Germany's iron and steel. The metals are used to make automobiles and trucks, industrial and agricultural machinery, ships, and tools. The Ruhr region also makes chemicals and **textiles**.

Germany is the third-largest manufacturer of automobiles in the world. Manufacturers also make cement, clothing, electrical equipment, and processed foods and metals. Its chemical industry produces medicines, fertilizers, and plastics. Other important products include cameras, computers, leather goods, scientific instruments, toys, wood pulp, and paper.

Germany still relies on coal as its major source of electrical power. But oil-burning and **nuclear**-power plants have become more common. Oil-burning plants depend on oil imported from the Middle East. Southern mountain streams generate **hydroelectric** power.

Chemical plant in the Ruhr

Cities

Berlin, Hamburg, and Munich are Germany's largest cities. Berlin is Germany's capital and largest city. It is one of Europe's **cultural**, historical, political, and **economic** centers. It has many parks, lakes, gardens, and forests. It also has department stores, banks, hotels, cultural institutions, and theaters. Important museums, libraries, and historical memorials are located here.

Hamburg is Germany's second-largest city and most important industrial center. It is also one of the largest seaports on the European continent, and is one of Germany's leading railroad centers.

Hamburg's industries include chemical plants, ironworks, food processing, steelworks, sawmills, and shipbuilding. Many of Germany's industrial products, such as automobiles, machinery, and **optical** goods, are shipped from Hamburg.

Munich is Germany's third-largest city. It is a major transportation center that links northern and southern Europe. Munich is one of Germany's most important **economic** centers. Its industries include electronics, food processing, printing, publishing, and the manufacture of chemicals, machine tools, optical instruments, and **textiles**. Munich is also known for its breweries.

Boats and residences lining a waterway in Hamburg

Transportation & Communication

Trains and automobiles are the most important means of transportation in Germany. The country has one of the largest railroad networks in the world. Its road system includes 6,500 miles (10,500 km) of four-lane highways called *Autobahnen*.

Waterways also play an important role in transportation. The Rhine River and its branches carry more traffic than any other European river system. Canals connect Germany's major rivers.

Germany's largest airline is Deutsche Lufthansa. It flies to all parts of the world. Major airports are located in many cities, including Berlin, Düsseldorf, Frankfurt, Hamburg, Leipzig, and Munich.

Germany has about 400 daily newspapers. The largest is Hamburg's *Bild Zeitung*. Germany also has many public and private radio and television stations.

*Concrete stilts carry an **Autobahn** past a white-walled church and houses.*

Government

Germany is a federal **republic**. The government has a **parliament**, a federal **chancellor**, a federal president, and a **cabinet**.

Parliament has two houses, the *Bundestag* (Federal Diet) and the *Bundesrat* (Federal Council). The *Bundestag* passes laws and chooses the head of government. The *Bundestag* is the house in which Germany's 16 states are represented.

The federal chancellor is the head of Germany's government. The chancellor chooses the cabinet ministers and government department heads.

The federal president is the head of state. But this position is largely ceremonial. *Bundestag* deputies and the German state legislatures elect the president to a five-year term.

Each of Germany's 16 states has its own legislature. Members are usually elected to four-year terms. In most states, a minister president heads the state government. In the Berlin, Bremen, and Hamburg city-states, a mayor heads the government.

The German **Bundestag**

Holidays & Festivals

Most of Germany's cities and towns have festivals that celebrate music, film, and arts. The Bayreuth Festival is held each summer in northern Bavaria. It is dedicated to the performance of composer Richard Wagner's operas.

The oldest German festival is the Passion Play. It is held every 10 years in southern Bavaria to celebrate the end of the **Black Death**. Berlin has five major festivals, including the *Berliner Festwochen* ("Berlin Festival Weeks") in September and October. Munich has an opera festival in July and August.

Pre-Lenten celebrations known as *Fasching* are held in the Catholic and Protestant southern regions. *Karneval* is held in the Rhineland. Both feature parades and costumes. Major religious festivals include Easter, Christmas, and Whitsun, which are also national holidays. Another important national holiday is Unity

Day on October 3. It celebrates the reunification of East and West Germany.

Local celebrations include wine festivals, beer festivals, harvest festivals, hunting festivals, and historical festivals. Munich's Oktoberfest is held every September.

A beer hall during Oktoberfest

Sports & Leisure

Germany's varied landscape is ideal for outdoor activities. Canoeing, rowing, sailing, and swimming are popular on Germany's many lakes and rivers. Skiing and hiking are favorite sports in the mountain regions. Some young people carry knapsacks and spend the night outdoors or at inexpensive inns called youth hostels. Many Germans also enjoy reading, gardening, and watching television.

Soccer is the most popular organized sport in Germany. Thousands of soccer teams represent German towns or cities. Gymnastics, tennis, track, and sharpshooting clubs are also popular.

Germany has produced some of the world's greatest musicians and writers.

Ludwig van Beethoven

Johann Sebastian Bach and Ludwig van Beethoven are two of the world's greatest music composers. Writers Johann Wolfgang von Goethe and Thomas Mann are recognized for their great literary works. More recently, German scientists have made breakthroughs in chemistry, medicine, and physics.

Berlin has many important museums. Museum Island has the National Gallery, the Pergamon Museum, and the Bode Museum. Other museums are found throughout the city.

The German Museum in Munich is famous for its technology and science exhibits. An opera house, the Hagenbeck Zoo, and many museums are located in Hamburg.

The Berlin Philharmonic is one of the world's great orchestras. Important film directors from Germany include Percy Adlon, Doris Dörrie, the Polish-born Agnieszka Holland, Michael Verhoeven, and Wolfgang Petersen.

Glossary

academics - subjects taught in school, such as reading, writing, and arithmetic.

allies - countries that agree to help each other in times of need. During World War II, Great Britain, France, the United States, and the Soviet Union were called the Allies.

Black Death - a deadly disease that spread throughout Europe between 1347 and 1351.

cabinet - a group of advisers chosen by the chancellor to lead government departments.

chancellor - the chief minister of state in some European countries.

communism - a social and economic system in which everything is owned by the government and given to the people as needed.

concentration camp - a camp where political enemies and prisoners of war are held. During World War II, many Jews were sent to concentration camps in Germany and Poland.

coniferous - a type of tree that has needles or cones, and does not lose its needles in the winter.

culture - the customs, arts, and tools of a nation or people at a certain time.

democracy - a governmental system in which the people vote on how to run the country.

denomination - a religious group or sect.

dictator - a ruler who has complete control and usually governs in a cruel or unfair way.

dynasty - a series of rulers who belong to the same family.

economy - the way a city or nation uses its money, goods, and natural resources.

escarpment - a steep slope or cliff.

hydroelectric - the kind of electricity produced by water-powered generators.

nuclear - of or relating to atomic energy.

optic - of or relating to vision or the eye; the lenses, mirrors, or light guides of an optical instrument or system.

parliament - the highest lawmaking body of some governments.

plateau - a raised area of flat land.

prime minister - the highest-ranked member of some governments.

republic - a form of government in which authority rests with voting citizens and is carried out by elected officials such as a parliament.

Roman Empire - the empire of ancient Rome, extending from Britain to North Africa to the Persian Gulf. Emperor Augustus began the empire in 27 B.C. and it lasted until A.D. 395, when it split into the Eastern and Western Roman Empires.

textile - of or having to do with the designing, manufacturing, or producing of woven fabric.

vocational - of or relating to training in a skill or trade to be pursued as a career.

Web Sites

Germany Tourism—http://www.germany-tourism.de
Visit Germany's rivers, cities, and national parks at this site from Germany's tourism board. Virtual tours, events, and more can be found at this informational site.

German Embassy—http://www.germany-info.org/f_index.html
Get current news from the German Embassy in Washington, D.C. Learn about German culture, economy, and government.

Eltz Castle—http://www.burg-eltz.de/e_index.html
Explore Eltz castle, one of Germany's most beautiful castles. Castle tours and a treasure vault await your visit!

These sites are subject to change. Go to your favorite search engine and type in Germany for more sites.

Index